God, Jesus, Christ - History Here on Earth

God, Jesus Christ His Story Hear it on

Earth

I0467624

Pastor Steven Bates

The Table of Contents

Introduction

Jesus Christ, History Here on Earth. Jesus Christ (His Story – Hear about it)

on Earth.

This book is about Lord and Savoir Jesus Christ. I am an ordinated

Christian Pastor and I studied the Holy Bible I searched for hidden

messages. As the bible was recorded thru the fall of The Roman Empire

words dev eloped multiple meanings, The Holy Bible is often called the

Good Book. The Gospels to a non Enlish spealer may sound like Good

Spell , which could mean good writings Or good news. Using this concept

along with learning some History , one can develop a better

understanding of Christians , Jews and World Economics. The parts of this

book can lead a person to history and technology and more some will

think of Science Fiction while other think real science . Just like the title

some will think of here on Earth will other use the synonym or homonym

hear like they hear the good news with their ears. While others hear the

word here like a location.

Chapter 1

The Holy Bible

The Whole Buy Bill

Donald Trump will be America's president. He is a successful

businessman. The world today is control buy capitalism; North and South

America, Europe and Australia are mostly Christian. The Christians and

Jews have purchased the continents of North and South America, Europe

and Australia. English is the worlds must important language. The British

Empire ruled the world in the 1800's and the USA in the 1900's. The King

James Version of the Holy Bible was published in the 1600's. Language is

important in for Christians once the Catholic mass was given in Latin but

that changed in the 1970's. Once mankind spoke one language and the built a tower up to heaven. God who is also Jesus Christ destroyed the tower and divided the languages of mankind. From the beginning Jesus Christ was here on Earth. He is the Father the son and the Holy Ghost. He spoke the world into being. He said let there be light and there was light. In the Holy Bible at Pentecost Jew s who spoke in languages that they did not know and was said to be full of the spirit. If a man from France was speaking with a man from the USA there are words that sound alike and or are spelled alike but have different meanings. Synonyms and homonyms. If the were talking about the Sun of God Jesus it may sound like the sun in the sky. After al Jesus Christ is a light to guide mankind. Jesus is gods only son so he is the sole heir. Those words in English Sole Heir for only inheritor sound like the French word soleil which means sun. Holy Bible says Jesus is King of Kings and Lord of Lords the British and American culture was headed by Christians. So presidents, prime ministers and kings recognized Jesus as the lord. The triumph of Christianity was purchased by the blood of Jesus Christ. Jesus It was purchased. In contemporary USA Accounting and Business law is impotent , contracts and legal services are needed. The Holy Bible says God made man in his own image . So when Jesus Christ died on the cross for the sin of mean, he gave himself as a living sacrifice to god who he is also. The

Father the Son and the Holy ghost are the4 same how can this be? God said in Greek he is the Alpha and Omega . The beginning and the end. Jewish physicist Albert Einstein said if some one travels fasters then light the can travel time. Since god invented light he can go faster then it. So in science fiction novels and the Big and small movie and television screens have time travel shows mankind dreams of Science Fiction but with God it's science fact. Sci fi speaks of multiple dimension and time warps. For god it's magic and magic sounds like machine so god who is the Trinity the Father the Son and the Holy Ghost one time warp Jesus was God, the using a time machine which may sound like time magic to a speaker of another language god revised time and begin it again as a human on earth is himself and his son than after the death on the cross he reversed time again time warped it an came to Earth as the Holy Ghost. Therefore God which also sounds like good and guide and God – Jesus Christ is good and a guide to mankind . Purchased the world and the Holy Bible is the Whole Buy Bill of Bill of sales to how Jesus Christ purchased the world. Jesus , Yahweh and Jehovah or the same word spelled just different languages like German and English. By the 1500's Europe discovered the New World. The protestant reformation against the Roman Catholic church begin. The pope of Rome divided North and South America and Africa between Spain and Portugal . The war of the Protestant Reformation raged in Europe in the name of Jesus Christ Europe was at war. The Spanish where conquering the Native American Indians and converting them to Roman Catholic Church. Also the Portuguese was enslaving black Africans taking them to South America . Other Europeans where also enslaving black African and bringing to North and South America. The fact that were slaves long ago in Egypt north east Africa did not prevent the black African slave trade. History has a habit of repeating itself in a why. The Protestant Reformation was started by a man call Martin Luther, In it changed North and central Europe. And the invention of the printing press made the Holy Bible available to everyone. It was printed in other languages not just Latin. In America the was a civil war that lead to the end of slavery in the USA and to save the USA as a land of freedom to the whole world. Abraham is known as the father of the Jews to show has loyalty he was ready sacrifice his son as a living sacrifice to god. And in time god gave his son to the World as a living sacrifice to the world. Another Abraham who is Abraham Lincoln freed the Black slaves of the USA and kept the USA together . So black Americans who are mostly Christian have an Abraham to be thankful to like the Jews. Also in the USA More freedom and full rights of citizenship in the USA and a powerful force for what is known is the civil rights movement was Dr. Martin Luther King jr. so Black Americans have a Christian leader named Martin Luther just like the Protestants of Europe and the rest of the world. Jesus lived on the Earth and world history in North and South America , Europe Australia and other places is the history of Jesus Christ. Since the 300's AD when the Roman Empire legalized Christianity , and god truly purchased the Roman world with Jewish and Christian cultere , the faith has been a powerful social , political force and lifestyle through the world.

Chapter 2

The Old Testament

The Old Test of Man

Mankind reached a height during the Roman Empire . Rome controlled

the entire Mediterranean sea. The lands of what was the Egyptian and

Greek Empires as well is Israel was now the Roman Empire. The Latin

language was the language of the Romans . Earlier in history God who is

also Jesus Christ amd the Holy Ghost , destroyed the Tower of Babel.

When the Roman Empire was destroyed in the 300's by the Germanic

invaders the Roman Empire had become a Christian Empire. Jesus Christ

as God of the Holy Trinity was born and raised in Asia and Africa. Jesus

Christ was tested, by follow Jews also Greeks and Romans. Some

demanded him to perform miracles to prove he was the son of God.

Jesus Christ was like a Medical Doctor . He traveled around curing people

of their mental and physical illnesses. But many Jews and others called

him a fraud. In the Old Testament book of Ezeikiel God turned dead

bones into living creatures , so when Jesus Christ returned the dead

people back to life many times , the Jews were already familiar with this type of magic. Jesus Christ was testing man kind as he saved mankind. A great test of man or New Testament was when God told Noah to build the Ark. Noah warned has neighbors and warned them of the up coming flood but he was mocked and ridiculed. Then the world was destroyed . However God said he would never destroy the world like that again. Mankin d was tested by water with Noah. It rain for 40 days. Mankind was tested by God when Moses pated the Red Sea as he lead the Jews out of slavery in Egypt, and drowned the Egyptian military that was attempting to bring them back to slavery in Egypt of the leaders of Egypt changed their minds on letting the Jews go free to their promised land. Although the Jews passed an Old Test of Man by escaping Egypt they would wonder in the desert for 40 years, before reaching their promised land of Canaan . In Canaan the land of Israel was established , some one speaking old English or an other language may think they hear the phase issued real estate. Because God Issued the real estate of the Canaan's to the Jews that were fleeing Egypt. When God came to Earth as Jesus Christ he returned to Egypt for a while. King was working with the Romans an ordered you boys to be killed in Israel . This was not the first time the Jews had heard of such things. Once Jesus Christ who is also God and the Holy Host sent an angel to kill many in Egypt . This was celebrated as the

Jewish Passover , and preceded the Roman Empire. God came to earth as a human during the Roman Empire . God came to Earth as an infant . Man have been tested since the Garden of Eden. When man could not resist a women's tempting or the desire to be smart and knowledgeable like God. After all man were made in Gods image. In the 1900's a Jewish scientist Albert Einstein explained through Physics that a vessel I going past the speed of light can travel time. In the New Testament it says 1 day is like a thousand years to God. The Old Testament says God made the world in 6 days. So that could mean 6,000 years. Then he rested for a day. That's a thousand years. As he traveled the world as the Holy Ghost he could have traveled faster than light and came to Earth an influence the development of mankind. The theory of Gods as not just Jewish and Christian . The Greeks , Romans , Egyptians and others had Gods. But their religious books could not match the Old Testament, The Old Testament is full of History and Political Science and Economics. After the temple was destroyed in Jerusalem in 70 ad. The Jew settled throughout the Roman Empire and the Old Testament gave them an advantage, The used the Economic theories of the Old Testament to help them became a powerful force in business world of the Roman Empire. They would become the importers and exporters of nations, Jews in Greece would trade with

Jews in Egypt and they would share their Jewish faith and become

wealthy business people business was part of the Torah. The Jews had a

self esteem, Their faith told them they were the chosen people of God.

With such an advantage it's wonder Jewish scientist of the 1800's and

1900's Karl Marx , Albert Einstein and Sigmund Freud. Would develop

Communism , Psychology and Physics. The Old test od man is night just

ancient history, the Old Testament is full of prophets . And prophets

sound like profits and Jews are known to make profits in the business

world up until the second would war , the holocaust and killing of 6

million Jews and the establishment of modern Israel in 1948. In the old

testament God who is Jesus Christ and the Holy Ghost destroyed the

cities of Sodom and Gomora . With fire from the sky. Since the Greeks

and Alexander the Great in the BC's to Napoleon the first of France the

militaries of the world wanted such power then during world war 2 The

USA invented and used the Atonic bomb , using theories of the Jewish

scientist Albert Einstein , one Aton Bomb could destroy a whole city.

Adolph Hitler Nazi Germany who wanted to kill all Jews in Europe military

ally Japan was bombed twice with Atomic Bombs ending World War 2,

After World War 2 Jewish economist theory of communism was the law

of the USSR and Eastern Europe the USA fought the Communist in Korea and Vietnam. Communism ended in the USSR and Europe in the 1990's,

However a form of Karl Marx Communism still exist in the powerful I

nation of the Peoples Republic of China.

Chapter 3

The New Testament

The New Test of Man

The New Testament in the Holy Bible begins with the birth of Jesus Christ.

God came to earth as a human. He was born of a virgin mother. It also

begins in the Roman Empire. When God came to Earth as Jesus Christ he

challenged humanities highest culture up to that time. The Roman

Empire. In the 1800,s it was said Britain ruled the waves. During the

Roman Empire the Mediterranean Sea was rule by the Roman naval fleet.

Ports that after Columbus discovered the New World in 1492 would

launch ship to colonize North and South America and enslave black

Africans The enslavement of black Africans ended in the 1880's when

Brazil abolished slavery. Portuguese off shoot Brazil was a child of the

Roman Empire. Along with France , Spain and Britain these former

sectors of the Ramon Empire built New sea borne Empires that would

rival the splendid , wealth and power of Roman, while Rome itself would

fall asleep. Italy would not unite into a country until the late 1800's. Mans

New Test was if mankind would welcome God. In the Roman Empire man

killed Jesus Christ after all his magical displays of super natural powers,

the Jews and Romans where unimpressed and killed Jesus Christ.

However Jesus Christ new that would happen and so did the Old

Testament prophets . Jesus Christ said he was the Alpha and the Omega

the beginning and the end. The world had already happened before and

God was is also the Father and the Holy Ghost depending on the time warp and dimension knew what would happen. Mankind reached a new height as Europe conquered the world. The Roman Catholic Church was powerful in Europe and the New World Native Americans also known as Indians were being converted to the Roman Catholic Church. The Spanish wanted gold for the crown and souls for Jesus Christ. The Europeans justified the enslavement of Black Africans buy quoting verses in the Holy Bible that said slaves should respect their masters as while as other quotes. It would not be until the 1950's when a Black American Christian preacher Martin Luther King jr. would begin to use the Christian faith to liberate the Black people of the USA. A hundred years after the USA's civil war ended leading to the end of black slavery in the USA black Americans were second class citizens and denied full rights as citizens of the USA. Jesus Christ was called the prince of peace. The Holy Bible is full of was but it is said man will turn their swords into farming instruments . Todays swords are powerful, H – bombs that only takes one bomb to destroy an entire city. Man kind had its greatest test in history during the second world war. The Europeans destroyed each other. The Nazi Germans sought to eliminate the Jewish population of Europe. The European white race had ruled the world since the 1500's. But that begin to change with the Russian – Japanese war in the early 1900's and the Japanese continued to build their military until they rivaled the militaries of European nations. Also the USA defeated Spain during the Spanish American war in the late 1800's. The Europeans destroyed them selves in the first world war. The war displayed the barbarian ways of the civilized Europeans. But it was the second world war where to really test the man of Europe when Adolph Hitler and The Nazis ruled Germany. They said that the Germans where an Aryan master race, destined to rule the world in a 1000 year empire. The threat to their empire war the Jews inside Germany and the inferior Slavic races to the east where Germany needed to rule if they wanted to survive. After 6 years of war the Nazis were defeated, Man king displayed god like powers, like mosses parting of the Red Sea the Allies in 1944 crossed the English Channel freeing western Europe from the Nazis. The Russians would free the East of Europe from the Nazis. And start half a century of being a Cold War superpower using the Economic and Political Science of Marxism mixed with some Leninism to create a communist empire. The second world war ended when 2 Atomic Bombs were used against Japan in 1945. The Japanese were a Yellow race and almost conquered the world and Adolph Hitler Nazism destroyed racism in Europe . The British , French , Dutch . Belgium ,

Portuguese and others last there philosophy of racial supremacy. Also the communist Russians or the USSR were aiding independence movements against European colonies in Africa and Asia. After the second world war the world was under an Economic war because white Americans and Europeans did not fight face to face but other races of the world it was known as the Cold War. As Jesus Christ walked the world be the Father , the Son and the Holy Ghost all at once he is omnipotent and everywhere at once. The witnessed the Death Camps of Nazi Germany, but during World War 2 by the German homes were death camps as the Allies bombed German cities day and night. In Dresden creating such heat there were fire tornadoes . And in Japan Hiroshima and Nagasaki were Atomic bombed , one bomb destroying an entire city. People would call World War 2 Total War. Woman and children were killed as well as the military. Christian leaders would preach to the world that God would judge man, however IN the 1940's man also judged themselves. The were trials in courts in Nuremberg were Nazis where charged   with among other things , Crimes Against Humanity . In in 1920's USA there were the Scopes – Monkey trail in the states of Tennessee USA where Evolution being taught in schools instead of the Holy Bible was put on trail. Jesus Christ is the Justice Courts. Also in the Middle Ages after the fall of the Roman

Empire Justice Courts and Jesus Christ meant about the same thing. And

Sheriff meant share wealth because the Jewish 10 Commandments & the

Holy Bible was shared with Europe, And the Sheriff symbol often

resembles the Jewish Star of David.

Chapter 4

Jewish Science

Today there are Mass Media . Radio , Television and the Internet and

World Wide Webb. In the 1500's the invention of the printing press

revolutionized mass media of that era. Now books that had to be produced independently by a scribe could be mass produced . Also around that era the Protestant Reformation lead to the use local languages in education. At that time literature allowed science to evolve , now that science could share information. Also the Roman Catholic Church no longer controlled education. Until the Renascence the Roman Catholic Church banned many sciences . The only place to find science was the The Greek , Hebrew and Latin Holy Bible. The Roman Catholic Church was a major part of the Whole Buy Bill of Western and Northern Europe. Language is important in the Holy Bible. In the Old Testament God spoke the world into existence. In the New Testament the first 4 books are called the Gospels . This word branches off to many other phases and meanings . Such as the Good Spelling or Good writing also Gods spelling or Gods writing , As the Torah would guide the Jews as well as later Gentiles Gospel means Guided Spelling or Guided writing . As the Roman Catholic Vatican was arresting scientist who said the world was round and revolved around the Sun. The Jews still had the science of the Torah and Old Testament. After the Germanic invasions of the Roman Empire the Roman Catholic Church would maintain a form of government and civilization in lands that would become Portugal , Spain , France England and Italy among others. One of the reasons the Jews would become good in Business and Science was the Jews had annual holidays that where very important to them also they could only work 6 days a week . So they rabbis studied the skies , the moon , the sun and the stars. What the Greeks called Astrology and horoscope had its Jewish equal valance. The Jews kept notes and had religious rules and regulations concerning owning land, and performing business transactions. In the New World of the USA after Black slavery was ended America was conquering the Native American Indians and taking all land in North Americans for the White man. slavery was ended the land was now the most valuable commodity. Many Jews left Europe and came to the USA. They did well in Real Estate and became know as a race of land owners and land lords. Also Jews traded with each other from country to country being importt and export specialist. Where ever the Jews went in Europe and the USA they were good in Real estate and business thanks to the traditions of the Torah and Holy Bible to t6hings like real estate laws and business laws rules and regulations. About the mid and late 1800's the Old and New Test of Man or Old and New Testaments were going full scale . New Sciences were evolving . The slave trade on black Africans ended in the 1880,s in Brazil but the second wave of European colonization of the world begin. France , Britain , Portugal , and newly united Germany Colonized Africa and Asia. The Former North and South American Colonies of the Spanish , the Portuguese and Britain among other were free nations since the early 1800's. New science would flourish in the 1800's Charles Darwin's theory of Evolution . In the Jewish scientists Karl Marx was explaining Economics to the world and laying the foundations of communism. In the early 1900's the world was rule by the USA and European empires.   The USA beat the Spanish and the Yellow Japanese beat Russia. Therefore as the first world war loomed it was known being White or European no longer meant one would be the military leader. Although might makes right no longer was whites are always the ones with might. In 1914 world war one begin. At about that time Man had planes and could fly in the air. They head cars and submarines. The first submarines were used i8n the 1860's during the American Civil War. During that war some promised the freed black African slaves land and or transportation back to Africa. However that would never happen. By the time of the first world war the German Empire had a colonial empire and its navy was growing they were catching up the the British navy, During the war the German submarines called u-boats were sinking ships trading with the British. Although there was cultural heritage the USA claimed neutrality. But in 1915 an American ship with civilians on it was sunk. And lead to the USA involvement in world war 1 in 1917. In 1917 the Germans were driven out of their 4 African colonies by the British. Also the monarchy of Russia was over thrown and Lenin would establish the USSR a country bases on some of Karl Marx's philosophy . When world war 1 ended people questioned the civilization of man a new science called Psychology was developing. Jewish pioneers of Psychology like Sigmund Fraud and Eric Erickson became popular. Also Jews used the new technology of film and movie projectors to develop Hollywood , and make what would be called magic. And actors and actresses would be called stars, Because people looked up to them like stars in the sky. One movie It's a Wonderful Life had a time traveling angel. Jewish scientist Albert Einstein explained time travel although mankind can not time travel that's still Hollywood fantasy man can destroy an entire city with 1 Hydrogen bomb, using Albert Einstein physics theory. And from 1045 until 1991 Jewish Scientist Karl Marx's based Communism would rule Russia and Eastern Europe as the USSR. After World War 2 was over the United Nations was created. years of it's forming the British who ruled Israel then . Give Israel to the United Nation and the United Nation Made it a nation. Only 1 few years after 6 million

Jews were killed by Nazis. The Jews had had back Israel , their issued real

estate . Also part of Jerusalem. Jerusalem means Jew Rule Some Land.

Chapter 5

Black Christians

The majority of Blacks in the USA are Christians. Many Blacks go to

church on Sundays and sing praises to God who is also Jesus Christ and

the Holy Ghost. Some dance and shout and are said to be full of the Holy

Ghost. Black Christians in the USA have been singing praises to Jesus

Christ since the days of slavery. Before the Civil War it was illegal for

Blacks to learn to read. Blacks heard about the word of God the Good news of Jesus Christ orally and sung about Jesus Christ while picking cotton and other chores. Today Black American Gospel Music is a significant part of the USA multi - i billion dollar music industry. After the Civil War when slaves were free they mostly read the Holy Bible. Black Christian preachers became prominent members of Black society in the USA. IN 1954 when the US Supreme Court rule Separate but Equal in Schools was un constitutional the Civil Rights Movement began . Soon Rev Martin Luther King jr. would became the main leader of Black America and the Civil Rights Movement. Black Americans related to the Jews in the Holy Bible because they had been slaves like the Black Americans. USA president Lindon B. Johnson sign the Voting and Civil rights acts and Rev Martin Luther king jr was there beside him. Later in the 1980's Reverent Jesse Jackson ran for President . Than in the 2000's Reverent Al Sharpton. Then in 2008 **Barack Obama was elected President of the USA. Black Christians were also important in other parts of the world. In the 1990'2 Roman Catholic Priest Jean Bertacnd Aristide became president of Haiti . And in the 1980s Anglican Arch Bishop Desmond Tutu was an important leader of the South African anti Apartheid Movement. Jesus Christ Is Imporant to Blacks aroun the world but not all Black worshippers are Christian. IN Africa and the USA** some Blacks are Moslem. The Moslem faith began in the 600's AD. Then the Arabs swept up from the Arabian peninsula and into North Africa were they remain today..And in their Holy book the Koran, which sounds like Co Run or Combined Rule as the Koran is a Combined rule of God and Man Jesus Christ is considered a prophet. The Holy Bible and the Koran are important to world culture. The Jews and Arabs are considered precious like precious stones. Jews sound like Jewels and Arabs like Rubies . Like Jews are Jewels and Arabs are a ruby. Black in the USA have a history Jesus Christ is History al Earth History is of Jesus Christ as the Father , Son and Holy Ghost he can travel time in become anyone in the world at any time. He is omnipotent . The Blacks in the USA faced racism around the world, In the 1930. The Nazi leader Adolph Hitler ruled Germany. In 1936 Germany hosted the World Olympics. Adolph Hitler give gold medals to the winners. But he refused to give medals to Black American Jesse Owens. Adolph Hitler wanted to prove Germans were the White Master Race by winning the most medals in the Olympics. Jesse Jackson ruined that plan. And also another Black American Joe Louis the Black boxing Champion in the USA would fight German boxer Max Schmeling a couple of times. Adolph Hitler and German minister of propaganda Joseph Goebbels s would use the times when Max Schmeling beat Joe Louis to prove that the Germans were the Mater race of the world. At the time Black Americans were being discriminated against because of their race in Germany . They were also discriminated against in their country the USA. The USA would go to war against Nazi Germany in 1941, Finally the USA military gave Black Americans the chance to prove themselves and fight in battle. The Black College the Tuskegee Institute was choses and Black American college students were train to learn to fly planes for the USA military. In the USA Airforce the Black Americans became know as the Tuskegee Airmen. They would prove themselves in North Africa and Europe as they fought against the German Airforce called the Luftwaffe . The Tuskegee Airmen would become one of the most decorated USA military groups of World War 2. And as the Black American Tuskegee Airmen were fighting the Nazis, the Nazis were killing Jews in their death camps. Adolph Hitler and the Nazi party believr that the Germans were the Whote master race and that the Jews in Germany was poisoning their pure blood and holding Germany back. The Nazis would kill 6 million Jews in World War 2. And back to Jesse Owens and the 1936 Berlin Olympic Games the Nazi Germans banned American Jews from participation in the Berlin Olympics. After the massacre of Jews in

Europe by the Nazi Germans which has become known as the Holocaust . The world was ready to give the Jews their own land again. And in 1948 Israel became a nation again . The Black Americans could relate to the Jews and the watched as nation after Black African nation and the Caribbean Sea became independent countries. But as Black African colonies where becoming independent nations the country of South Africa established Apartheid . Many peple would call Apartheid Neo-Nazism although a couple of decades early the European colonist had similar laws in place but after World War 2 the mood of the world had changed. And in the USA in the 1970's Black Americans begin being elected Mayors of major American Cities. And Black Music was breaking down the American and world cultural difference. Today in the USA Blacks are Going to college and participation in government , business and culture and almost every else in the USA , but Black Americas are still stereo typed as Criminals and on welfare ghetto dwellers and from the Urban areas the culture of Rap Music has emerged. And in Africa the Blacks countries have a large supply of raw materials such as gold, diamonds and Uranium . But the are still considered Third World and full of poverty.

Chapter 6

The End of Time

Some people call the book of Revelation the news of the end of times.

Jesus Christ was here on Earth in the beginning and in the end as

the Holy Ghost and omnipotent God he could through time travel

with magic which also means machines built by angels god could

be anywhere or anyone at the same time as science fiction novels

and films but this supernatural and from God. In the last book of

the New Testament in the book of Revelation it explains that

near the end of time economics would change. A power called the

Beast will arise and people will not be able to buy or sell or do business with out the mark of the Beast on their foreheads and the back of their hands. And the number 666 will be used Over the centuries and through multiple time warps this part of Revelation was interpreted and performed differently. At one space and time The end of time did not mean the end of history but the end of the week or the end of the day. In present time USA and the UK among others countries on Friday nights people gather in night clubs . To do business or enter the clubs, they must hold out their hand with an identification card in it and often receive a mark on their hand. Also The identification they submit will have their face showing their forehead. And many clubs or for adults and they must be 18 and 6 + 6+ 6 equals 18 which is the age of adulthood in the USA. Also in another dimension of time the book of Revelations explains the erase of the Dragon. In todays world people often think of China when they hear dragon . The Mark of the Beast can be interpreted By some as the manufacturing of Beijing . Many businessmen in the USA need Chinese whose capital city is Beijing factories or manufacturers to make their products. Without China some businesses could not succeed . The Cold War has ended . Karl

Marx Communism exits only in China , North Korea and Cuba.

However China is growing into a new superpower and North

Korea has Nuclear weapons. As the USSR and the Warsaw Pact in

Eastern Europe fall apart in the 1990's the world rejoiced that

Nuclear Holocaust Between the USA and the USSR was over

MADD or Mutually Assured Destruction and Nuclear Winter and

War and the end of Mankind was over. But as the Nuclear threat

to mankind was reducing new plagues and diseases were

evolving . A new disease that Medical Doctors deemed incurable

emerged. It was called AIDS or HIV. Some people say AIDS or HIV

is a divine punishment for Earths sins from Jesus Christ , who is

also God and the Holy Ghost. One race of people and Continent

has been hit the hardest. Africa. In the Old Testament god sent

plagues to Egypt which is in Africa. Blacks in Sub Saharan Africa.

Has the worlds highest percentage of AIDS in the world. And also

Haiti the Mostly Black racially and the poorest country in North or

South America has the highest rates in North and South America.

It's a disease mostly spread through sex. Todays Medical Doctors

can not cure AIDS. So AIDS has become a death sentence. And

people with HIV and AIDS are sometimes called the living dead.

Jesus Christ brought the dead back to life in the New Testament.

Also in the book of Ezekiel in the Old Testament. When Jesus

Christ rose from the dead many called it a good miracle from god.

In todays world people fear the supernatural, because modern

science has not proven that there is life after death or ghost the

word for dead people coming back to like is zombie and in todays

world only are discussed in horror movies. People like to use

initials to stand for things and if people searching for hidden

meaning in the English language HIV and AIDS and can mean

Haitian Island Voodoo and AIDS African Invisible Demon Spirits .

Since a lot of AIDS in the past and HIV was passed thru sex AIDS

and HIV is called a Venereal Disease. VD can mean Voodoo or

Venereal Disease. Man has dominion over the Earth since the

Garden of Eden. Now after a few centuries of Industrialization

dust and green house effect have occurred as man kind uses fossil

fuels to run the cars, homes and industries. Now that the threat

of mankind ending in Nuclear Winter after a Nuclear war now the

actions are heating the planet and Polar ice capes are melting.

Scientist are warning this will lead to port cities around the world flooding. Now man is showing he can destroy the world with water lake God did with Noah's ark. Also today man can preserve a male and female member of almost every animal like on Noah's Ark by freezing fertilized embryos for later artificial insemination . Also Christians know God came Earth as Holy Ghost and Mary became pregnant and through a time travel the king man uses in Science Fiction movies and films God came back to earth as the baby Jesus Christ. Now medical doctors inject sperm through a needle into a virgins uterus and 9 months later a baby is born and they will call it a virgin birth. Toady man don't have time machines that's science fiction but supernaturally That will be a begging of a life and Jesus Christ Knows what kind of life that baby will have. So there is the Old Test of Men and New Test of Men, And the Whole Buy Bill which also mean Old Testament , New Testament and Hole Bible. when Jesus came back to life and showed doubting Thomas the holes in his hands and side some began calling God and Jesus Christ the Holey Ghost because of the holes Jesus Christ bore on his hands , feet and side.

Chapter Seven

Christian and Jewish Warriors.

In the last book of the Holy Bible it describes a war at Armagaden , In these war the armies of the world would fight against Israel. War is nothing new to the Holy Bible.Thru out the Old Testament there are wars . Some wars were cold without actual fighting and some ware cold. The Jews were in Egyptt for centuries but didn't have a home of their own. And they were treated like second class citizens. When the Jews finaly left Egypt they did not have to fight Moses lead them across the Red Sea. The Jews did not have to swim or use boat, The Jewish God parted the Red Sea. When the Egyptian army tried to pursue then the the Red Sea closed and the Egyptians were drowned. Also later in the Holy Bible The Jews were at war with Jericho, Also then they would not have to fight . They were told to circle the city a couple of times then blow their musical horns. When they blew their horns the wall of Jericho came tumbling down. The last war the Jews fought wars during or before the Roman

Empire. That was the last time they would have a nation of their own until

1948. In 1948 the United Nation granted Israel nation statues but

neighboring Arab nation declared war on Israel. Israel won, but didn't

control Jerusalem. Another Jewish Arabic war was in 1967 the Jews

captured Jerusalem. Then the was a war in 1973. On the Jewish Holiday

of Yum Kipper , the Jews stopped working including military to celebrate .

Some Arabic states Including Egypt which has been an Arabic state since

the 600,s invaded Israel . The Jews would win that war. Egypt and Israel

would sign a peace treaty in the late 1970's. At that time the USA under

Billy Carter had just finished the Vietnam war. Karl Marx was a Jewish

economist in the 1800's The USSR under a Marxist government would

control of half of the world while the USA would control the free capitalist

world, The Christian Wars would begin when the pagan Germanic tribe

like the Lombards , Vandals Visi Goths and Ostro Goths would conquer

the Christian Roman Empire. After that there would be the Dark Ages

when there would be small kingdoms and Pricipilities and Knights in

Shining armor battling each other , Also durind that time the Germanic

Vikings would sweep out of Scandanavia and pillage parts of Europe , The

last Gernaanic Invaders of the Roman Empire was the Anglos Saxons and

Jutes invading the British Ilse. A new era in Christian warfare would begin when Spain discovered Americ and Drove the Moors out of Spain., The Leader of the Roman Catholic Church would devide the Newly discovered would between Spain and Portugal . The Spanish warriors the Conqistadors wanted to get gold for the Spanish royal Crown and save souls for the Roman Catholic Church. The Spanish navy would have to fight pirates ships some backed by England who would intercept Spanish Ships full of gold from the conquered Inca's Mayas and Aztecs and other Native Americian also Known as Indians in the New World, The The British , Frnch Spanish , portudese and Dutch would fight wars twith each other over the colonies and slave trade. The Dutch conquered what is now New York City and the Spice Islands in South East Asia todays Indoniesia , The Brtitish and French fought a war over French royalty becoming rulers of the Spanish Throne. In important part of the Anglo fraco wars was the Qubec act where French Canadians could keep their French Language Toady Quebec is a a modern 1 st world French Speaki9ng part of North America . In Europe the Protestant Reformation lead to wars across the European continent. Also in the later 1700's the would be American and French Revolutions. Napoleon for over a decade leading his Armies from Russia to Egypt. The British would destroy

Napoleons navy of the coast of Egypt. Napoleons government would give independence to the mostly black island of Haiti and would its west of the Mississippi North American Colony during what is called the Lousianna Purchas. Also the USA and Britain had thir last war during the war of 1812. The USA would have peace until they fought a war with Mexico in the 1840's Then in the 1860's The southern States of the USA would leave the Union and form the Confederate States of America. In that Civil war which lasted 1861 to 1865 the USA was restored to one nation and the Black slaves were freed. All these wars fought in Europe and the North and South Americans were fought among major Christian nations of the time, being a Christian didn't mean peace. When the European Christians first ventured out of Europe it was during the Crusades.to free the Holy Land and Jerusalem from the Moslems . During on Crusade Children were sent as warriors in the belief that God would not let5 an army of Children loose a battle. The Children lost and most were sold into slavery. Today in the Christian world there are Children can't fight in wars most Americans are shocked when the see on television nations in Africa and Asia arming children in their armies. In the USA 18 year olds got the right to vote in the early 1970's. The average age of a Vietnamese soldier was 19. The Vietnam war war a proxy war between The USA lead Capitalist and Russian lead Communist. In what was the former French colony of French Indo China. During the early and Mid 1900's there where 2 great war . World War 1 and World War 2. In World war ! The British, French and Russians would fight a war with Germany and Austro-Hungary. Later the USA and the mostly Islamic Ottoman Empire would join the war. After World War One the Then after world war one Far Right Fascism and Comunism developed in Germany Italy and Russia, From 1939 tio 1945 The was the Europen war against Nazi Germany and Adolph Hitler. Hitler and the Nazis wanted to destroy the Jews in Europe and rule the world. After the end of World War 2 there was the Korean War where The USA and other Free Capitalist countries Fought The USSR and Communist China.

Chapter 8

Christian Technology

Todays high technology runs the planet earth with modern science fly an airplane from almost any two

nations in2 days. And with computers and various types of smart

telephones within minutes people can communicate t with each other from around the world. These technologies of airplane and computers

and telephones came to the world from inventers and scientist from

Europe and North America. Europe and North American are mostly

Christian so most modern technology can be described as Christian

Technology. How ever Christians have not always been fond of science.

After the fall of the Christian Roman Empire Europe fell into the Dark Age.

One of the only science was alchemy were scientist and magicians tried to

turn metals like lead into gold. This form of Chemistry was not supported

By the Roman Catholic Church. Alchemy and Chemistry was associated

with wicked witches brewing up magic potions . The was the Dark and

Middle Ages in Europe. How ever Europe would have the mostly Italian

Renaissance. The Roman Catholic supported the nation that the world

was flat and that the planet Earth was the center of the Universe. During

the Renaissance scientist developed telescopes and developed

Astronomy from Astrology , And scientist suggested that the Earth was

flat and that Earth revolved around the Sun. The Spanish in the late

1400's would develop the technology to build giant ships and the logistic

technology to travel from Europe to North and South America. These

giant ship could survive weeks and Months at sea , Later these giant sail

boats wouls need large cannons and weapons to fight pirates and each other. The most important development in weapons would be the knight in shining armor or the fight fighting with swords to the soldiers using muskets. And gun power was important for cannons and guns. One of the biggest development in ships was the slave ships which carried Black African slave from Africa to North and South America. The slaves were chained lying down on there backs for weeks or months. For centuries things stayed the same then there was the Industrial revelation in the 1800's. During this era the steam engine was developed and steam locomotives and giant steam ships were built and coal became a very important fuel, The development of the rail road open up distant lands. Someone good ride from New York the Western coast of North America in a few weeks. Also goods could be traveled from a distant place to another on a regular basis. The Technology of warfare developed in the 1800;, During the USA Civil War the machine gun and the submarine was developed. These invention be used half a century later in World War 1. The soldiers in Europe would fight in gas filled trenches with their machine guns. And the German Navy world attack the British navy with submarines. Also World War 1 would used the USA invented airplane as a weapon of war. Around 1903 the Wright Brothers invented the airplane. By that time the Morse code telegraph in use since the USA Civil War. In the late 1800's the Telephone, the Radio and the gasoline powered car would be developed. Dynamite would be developed as a weapon of war but it's inventor would develop the Nobel Prizes which gives annual awards in the fields of Chemistry, Pysics , Peace and other fields. During World War 2 most Europeans were Christian how ever there was a sizable Jewish population. Adolph Hitler and his Nazi German party would reign for 12 years. During those years they would kill 6 million Jews and destroy Parts of Europe such a London England with the world first Jet air planes. Also Surface to Surface long distance missiles and cruise missiles. At the end of World War 2 in 1945 the mostly Christian USA would end the war by dropping two Atomic Bombs. On Japan. Now the Christian world could destroy an entire city with one atomic bomb. After the Second World War Europe was divided between USA led Nato and West and Central Europe and USSR and Warsaw Pac t Eastern Europe. Karl Marx who was Jewish developed a form of Communism that would be used in The Russian USSR after World War 2. The USSR would challenge the worlds Capitalist free Enterprise system. After World War 2 the USA and the USSR captured Nazi German jet and rocket scientist . Than they fought for world supremacy in technology. During the Korean Conflict in the early 1950's The USSR and the USA fought a war and tested their jet fighters against each other. Then in 1957 the USSR built a space rocket and sent the artificial satellite into spance, This would set of a USA –USSR space race. After that the USSR would send a man into space orbit. By the Early 1960's President Kennedy who was a Roman Catholic would pledge to have the USA send a man to then have him safely return from the Moon. By 1969 the USA had completed this mission. At about that time in the 1960's . Almost all homes in the USA had televisions . radios and telephones. Also Cars and passenger airplanes were reliable sources of transportation. The rock bands like the Beatles could flu from Liverpool in England to New York City in a few hours. Also the the Beatles could record in album in England and hace it All over the radio and in record store in the USAs in a few weeks. Now it's 2017 or later and in the USA almost everyone has a potable Smart Phone or other device and participate in Facebook , twitter or other social media. The are also problems with Green House gases because of Carbons released from factories , and the exhaust from cars , trucks and other devices . It's at least 2017 and The USA has not found a cure for cancer or developed a car that drives it self or a reliable electric car, but Scientist are working on it. In 1991 the USSR and the Warsaw pact fell apart, Now all the world is Capitalist . China is in theory Communist but since the 1980's has allowed

Capitalist countries to invest in China. Now in 2017 China is second only to

the USAS in size of economy.

www.ingramcontent.com/pod-product-compliance
Lightning Source LLC
Chambersburg PA
CBHW051225170526
45166CB00005B/2046